Made in the USA
Monee, IL
24 July 2022

10242463R10070